D1630718

MAMA LOTTIES
TASTING THE MEDITERRANEAN
EXPLORING GIBRALTAR'S KITCHENS

Text and Photography copyright © Justin Bautista 2015

Mama Lotties Illustration by Amanda Breach - www.amandabreachillustrations.co.uk

Justin Bautista has asserted his right to be identified as the author of this Work in accordance with the Copyright, Design and Patents Act 1988 in the United Kingdom and in accordance with the Intellectual Property (Copyright and Related Rights) Act 2005 Sections 94 and 95 in Gibraltar.

THANK YOU
FOR YOUR AMAZING SUPPORT

FIND US ON
FACEBOOK

www.mamalotties.com

GET SOCIAL WITH US

SEARCH MAMA LOTTIES

CONTENTS

FEELING HUNGRY?

TOASTED ARTISAN BAGUETTE
WITH GARLIC & TOMATO
PAN CON AJO Y TOMATE

PADRON PEPPERS
WITH ROCK SALT

ROASTED PEPPERS
PIMIENTOS ASADOS

COLD TOMATO SOUP
MAMA'S GAZPACHO

MAMA'S
PULPO A LA GALLEGA

CHICKEN AND VEGETABLE BROTH
MAMA'S PUCHERO

SEASONED WITH PAPRIKA & CORRIANDER
SWEET POTATO CHIPS

GRIDDLE GRILLED PRAWNS
GAMBAS A LA PLANCHA
www.mamalotties.com

MAMA'S TUNA MAYONNAISE SALAD
MAMA'S ENSALADA DE ATÚN

MAMA'S SEAFOOD PAELLA

PATSY'S CALLOS

CABBAGE STEW
POTAJE DE COLES

BECHAMEL CROQUETTES
WITH LEFTOVER MEATS

HAM AND
PRAWNS LINGUINE

STUFFED FLANK STEAK
CIMA RELLENA

GRANNY'S CORDON BLEU
MAMA'S SAN JACOBO

GRANNY'S POOR MAN'S POTATOES
MAMA'S PATATA A LO POBRE

A SIMPLE CLAM & PASTA DISH
MAMA'S CLAM LINGUINE

AUNTY'S STUFFED PEPPERS
WITH MINCED MEAT IN A TOMATO SAUCE

HOT AND CREAMY
MUM'S PEPPERED STEAK

FRIED AND GLAZED RAISIN BITES
TORTILLAS DE PASAS

PASTELES DE
CABELLO DE ANGEL

SWEET FRIED FLAKE
HOJUELAS

SWEET EGG YOLK BALLS
YEMITAS DE HUEVOS

SWEET LIQUOR BISCUITS
BESOS

LIQUOR DRENCHED
ROSCO DE ANIS

MAMISA'S SWEET BREAD
PAN DULCE

WALNUT BREAD
PAN DE NUEZ

ALMOND TART
TARTA DE SANTIAGO

ALMOND LIQUOR FLAN
AMARETTO FLAN TRIFLE

STARTERS

PAN CON AJO Y TOMATE
TOASTED ARTISAN BAGUETTE WITH GARLIC & TOMATO

THIS RECIPE

SERVES 3

COOKING TIME
20 MINUTES

Love breakfast? Then you must enjoy it in true Mediterranean style, with plenty of tomato, garlic and olive oil. This meal, known locally as "Un Pipi" is especially enjoyed at brunch.

INGREDIENTS

- ARTISAN BAGUETTE OR PAN GALLEGA

- 4 LARGE TOMATOES

- GARLIC CLOVE

- VIRGIN OLIVE OIL

- ROCK SALT

LET'S COOK

1. There are two ways of cutting the baguette, It simply depends on your own preference. Either slice across into small round slices or as I prefer long and thin.

2. Toast your slices under a grill on a medium heat. Whilst the bread toasts, peel and slice the tomatoes and place them in a bowl, drizzle a little olive oil over it and crush into a puree.

3. Remove your toast from the grill and rub a peeled garlic all over, spread the tomato mixture over and season with a pinch of salt.

You can adjust the flavour to your liking, depending on how much you like garlic, salt or olive oil you wish to use.

MAMA LOTTIES - TASTING THE MEDITERRANEAN

PADRÓN PEPPERS
WITH ROCK SALT

THIS RECIPE
SERVES 2

COOKING TIME
5 MINUTES

I have always been a fan of peppers. This page and the next are one of my favourite ways of enjoying them. Simply fried and generously seasoned to perfection.

INGREDIENTS

- 10 ML VIRGIN OLIVE OIL
- 50 G PADRÓN PEPPERS
- COARSE ROCK SALT

LET'S COOK

This recipe is very simple and quick to do as the peppers are very easy to cook. We want to keep the fresh taste of the peppers and soften them.

1. First, in a large frying pan pour your oil and allow it to heat over a medium - high heat until you see the oil is excessively hot. *(It may start spitting or smoking)*

2. Carefully and gently place your peppers in the oil and stir around for a minute to quickly cook the skin of the peppers. Take extra care when doing this as the oil will most likely spit out of the pan.

3. Finally serve by sprinkling a large pinch of rock salt over your peppers.

PIMIENTOS ASADOS
ROASTED PEPPERS

THIS RECIPE
SERVES 2

COOKING TIME
1 HOUR 20

I enjoy this best when cold. The flavours of the gently roasted peppers and tomatoes with the crunch of the fresh, raw onion and drizzle of olive oil just tastes of the Mediterranean summer with every bite.

INGREDIENTS

- 1 LONG ROASTING RED PEPPER
- 1 LONG ROASTING GREEN PEPPER
- 2 LARGE TOMATOES
- OLIVE OIL
- VINEGAR (OPTIONAL)
- 1 MEDIUM SPRING ONION

LET'S COOK

1. Line an oven dish with foil paper and place the peppers and tomatoes, whole, inside the dish.

2. Roast in the oven at 200°C until you see one side of the pepper's and tomato's flesh is roasted. Turn these over and repeat on the other side. This can take up to an hour depending on your oven.

3. Once roasted remove from oven and place in a food bag or sealed container. This will allow the steam to continue to gently cook the peppers and tomatoes and separate them from the skin, making it easier for you to peel.

4. Peel the skin from the peppers and tomatoes and de-seed. Slice up your peppers and place in a terracotta bowl or ceramic dish.

5. Dress with plenty of oil and a couple of tablespoons of vinegar, if you desire a stronger taste. Thinly slice your spring onion to add some crunch and toss in with your salad.

MAMA LOTTIES - TASTING THE MEDITERRANEAN

MAMA'S GAZPACHO
COLD TOMATO SOUP

THIS RECIPE
SERVES 4

COOKING TIME
6 MINUTES

Mama has made this for as long as I remember and during the hot summer months you can find a fresh supply permanently in her fridge. This dish is full of flavour and goodness, all blended together and enjoyed as cold as possible.

INGREDIENTS

- 8 FRESH RED TOMATOES

- 2 FRYING PEPPERS

- 3 LARGE GARLIC CLOVES

- 1 MEDIUM GHERKIN

- 200 ML WATER

- 2 TBSP VINEGAR

- OLIVE OIL

- SALT

- CRUTONS *(OPTIONAL)*

LET'S COOK

1. Begin by peeling and de-seeding your garlic, peppers and gherkin. Once your vegetables are rinsed and clear of any seeds dice them up and place them in a large blender.

2. Blend together until you find everything is smooth. If you have some trouble and find it is too thick, top up with water and continue to blend until you are satisfied with the thickness.

3. Add a generous splash of olive oil, 2 tablespoons of vinegar and season with salt, blend together once more until you are satisfied with the taste.

4. Every person enjoys this differently so if you like this to be sharper add a little more vinegar. Finally serve with a few croutons and enjoy.

5. In total, this should make about one litre of soup, enough for four 250ml servings.

MAMA'S MARINATED OLIVES
CHILLI, GARLIC, LEMON AND CORIANDER

PREPARATION
10 MINUTES

Perfect to have on a dinner table to pick from between servings or to enjoy with friends alongside some drinks. Olives are so easy to marinate you can make your very own to suit your fancy.

INGREDIENTS

- 1 JAR OF PITTED OLIVES IN BRINE

- 4 SMALL FRESH CHILLIES

- LEMON

- 2 GARLIC CLOVES

- FRESH CORIANDER

- 100ML VIRGIN OLIVE OIL

LET'S COOK

1. Begin by draining the brine from the jar or tin of olives.

2. Cover these with olive oil and the zest and juice of half a lemon.

3. Very finely chop the garlic cloves, a small bunch of coriander and two of your fresh chillies and add these and the two whole chillies to the jar with your olives.

4. Seal your jar and flip over, shaking a few times to mix all ingredients together. Enjoy straight away or leave in the fridge to enjoy as you wish.

MAMA'S MARINATED OLIVES
MANCHEGO CHEESE AND SUNDRIED TOMATOES

INGREDIENTS

- 1 JAR OF PITTED OLIVES IN BRINE
- 1 JAR SUN-DRIED TOMATOES
- LEMON
- MANCHEGO CHEESE

LET'S COOK

1. Drain the brine from the jar of olives and place them in a bowl.

2. This recipe does not really have any measurements as it all depends on how much you want to blend the tastes of the ingredients.

3. Add 4 - 5 sun-dried tomato pieces to your olives, slicing them into small quarters.

4. Cut a large piece of manchego cheese, remember this is quite strong in flavour. Slice and dice your cheese into small chunks and throw in with the olives and tomatoes

5. Cover your olives with the 100ml of oil from the sun-dried tomato jar and mix together well.

6. Transfer everything into an airtight jar and leave it at least overnight in the fridge so the flavours can mix together, then enjoy as and when you wish.

MAMA'S PULPO
A LA GALLEGA

THIS RECIPE
SERVES 5
TAPAS

COOKING TIME
20 MINUTES

Simple, quick and satisfying. That is how I describe this octopus dish. Serve this as an apetiser for a large meal, alongside some 'Ensalada de Atún" and you have the perfect appetiser.

INGREDIENTS

- 3KG OCTOPUS *

- PIMENTON DULCE

- OLIVE OIL

- SEA SALT

* Make sure your Octopus has thick tentacles.

LET'S COOK

1. Begin by rinsing your octopus thoroughly under fresh water. Heat a large pan of water until you see it begins to simmer.

2. Grab your octopus by its head and dip it in and out of the hot water 3 times, *carefully doing so as I do not want you to burn yourself*. The aim is to cause the octopus' flesh to heat up and tense without breaking the skin.

3. After doing so, drop your octopus into the pan and leave to boil for about 35 - 40 minutes. The octopus should be soft and tender and not rubbery or tense, so make sure to check once in a while to be sure.

4. Remove the octopus from the pan and slice the tentacles thinly, in angles, spread them out onto a large dish and season with a generous amount of olive oil, pimenton dulce and a sprinkle of sea salt.

MAMA'S PUCHERO

CHICKEN & VEGETABLE BROTH

THIS RECIPE

SERVES 4

- - - - - - - - - - - - - -

COOKING TIME

50 MINUTES

There's always time for soup, Mama's Puchero is perfect for those winter nights in and even enjoyable on hot summer days. It's full of flavour which makes this the perfect starter.

INGREDIENTS

- TURKEY THIGH*

- HEN THIGH & DRUMSTICK*

- 200 G CHICKPEAS

- 3 CELERY STICKS

- 2 LARGE CARROTS

- 4 MEDIUM POTATOES

- SALTED BONES

- WATER

- SALT

- ANGEL HAIR PASTA OR RICE

1 KG of meat combined

LET'S COOK

1. Soak your chickpeas in water overnight before starting to cook this dish. Alternatively, you can use pre-soaked jarred chickpeas.

2. Peel and chop your celery and carrots to a size you are comfortable with. *I prefer mine as small cubes.*

3. Place the three ingredients above in a pressure cooker along with the turkey and hen pieces and fill with water, about 3/4 of the way. Leave to cook for 30 minutes.

4. After 30 minutes, and once the pressure has been reduced, rinse and add in the salted bones, *make sure to rinse these first though as they will otherwise make your soup way too salty and spoil it.* Add 4 peeled potatoes and cook until boiled and soft.

5. When soft, add your pasta and leave until ready. Make sure to taste and season your soup as necessary.

SWEET POTATO CHIPS

SEASONED WITH PAPRIKA & CORRIANDER

THIS RECIPE

SERVES 1

COOKING TIME

30 MINUTES

I'm a big fan of sweet potato, they have more nutrients than regular potatoes and twice the flavour. Sweet potatoes may be tough to slice but with a little effort, they are worth it.

INGREDIENTS

- 1 MEDIUM SWEET POTATO
- CAYENNE PEPPER
- SALT
- CORIANDER
- PEPPER
- OLIVE OIL

LET'S COOK

Preheat oven to 190 °C.

1. Rinse and slice your sweet potato into chips.

2. Transfer to an oven dish and drizzle generously with olive oil. Season with cayenne pepper, coriander, salt and pepper.

3. Place in the oven for 30 – 40 minutes until soft.

GAMBAS A LA PLANCHA
MAMA'S SIMPLY GRIDDLED PRAWNS

THIS RECIPE
SERVES 2

COOKING TIME
5 MINUTES

The simplest and messiest way to enjoy some langoustines have to be "a la plancha". Simply season, then peel away.

INGREDIENTS

- 8 LANGOUSTINES
  (4 PER PERSON)
- SEA SALT
- SPLASH OF OIL
- FRESH PARSLEY
- GARLIC

LET'S COOK

1. Thoroughly rinse your langoustines under fresh water. Meanwhile, turn on your hob to the highest setting and place a griddled pan over it.

2. Once the pan is extremely hot, carefully place your langoustines on top and season with a drizzle of oil and sea salt. As the pan is very hot, it may start to smoke.

3. Leave to cook for about 2 - 3 minutes until one side begins to char. Meanwhile, very finely, chop up a small bunch of fresh parley and garlic and mix with a drizzle of oil.

4. Flip over the langoustines and drizzle with your mixture, leave for another 2 minutes then serve.

5. Finish off by serving with a lemon wedge for those who want to squeeze-over some lemon.

MAMA'S ENSALADA DE ATÚN

MAMA'S TUNA-MAYONNAISE SALAD

THIS RECIPE

SERVES 7

COOKING TIME

25 MINUTES

Anytime, anywhere, with any meal. This salad is especially great when freshly prepared and served cold on a hot summer's day.

INGREDIENTS

- 1 KG NEW BABY POTATOES
- 4 EGGS
- 500 G PRAWNS
- 1 LARGE SPRING ONION
- 1 TUB MAYONNAISE
- 2 MEDIUM TINS TUNA
- 2 OR 3 LETTUCE LEAVES
- 1 LEMON
- OIL

LET'S COOK

1. Rinse and boil your baby potatoes, leaving their skin on. Once soft, easily scrape and peel their skin off. Dice and leave to one side.

2. Boil the eggs, this should take about 10 - 15 minutes depending on the size of the eggs. Once ready, set aside and allow to cool.

3. Boil the prawns whole, after around 3 - 5 minutes, remove and peel.

4. In a large bowl mix together your diced onion, potatoes, prawns, 3 eggs and drained tuna. Drizzle with oil and juice a lemon over everything.

5. Mix in 3/4 of the tub of mayonnaise and stir. Pour your mixture in a large dish and lay the lettuce leaves around.

6. Finish off by generously spreading a dollop of the remaining mayonnaise throughout and grating the remaining egg over everything.

MAINS

MAMA'S SEAFOOD PAELLA

THIS RECIPE

SERVES 6

- - - - - - - - - - - - - - -

COOKING TIME

1 HOUR 20

If you want a delicious fish Friday meal then this is most definitely the one. Heavenly with every bite, mama's seafood paella will leave you soaking up every last bit.

INGREDIENTS

- 6-8 TOMATOES
- 1 LARGE ONION
- 2 LONG FRYING PEPPERS
- 3 GARLIC CLOVES
- SAFFRON *(PINCH)*
- OLIVE OIL
- SALT
- BAY LEAF
- 500 G CLAMS*
- 500 G PRAWNS
- 2 MEDIUM SQUIDS
- RICE *(A HANDFUL PER PERSON + ONE EXTRA)*

*Soak your clams in water for a few hours before cooking to remove all sand.

LET'S COOK

1. Place a pan over a low to medium heat with a splash of olive oil and begin by making a refrito. Do this by finely dicing your onion and garlic and frying until translucent, then dicing your peppers and adding them to the pan along with your onions and garlic. Cook until soft.

2. Once soft, chop your tomatoes and add to the pan. Continue to gently fry until the tomato turns soft and begins to puree a little.

3. Meanwhile, rinse and peel the prawns, removing the tails, shells and heads.

Place the prawns to one side and throw the shells and heads into a separate smaller pan and cover with water. Boil this separate pan for 10 minutes to create a stock.

4. Meanwhile, slice your squid into little portions, *I like to keep the tentacles whole and slice the rest into chunks,* add this to the pan. Now add a generous pinch of saffron, bay leaf and the clams, cover with the water that you boiled the prawn shells in. Sieve and drain the water into your paella dish, and top up to cover your ingredients. Stew for about 10 minutes so that the squid becomes a little, but not completely tender.

5. Add the rice and top up with more water to cover the rice and leave to stew for 20 minutes, checking occasionally as the rice will soak up a lot of the moisture. Stir if required as we do not want the bottom to burn.

6. Add the peeled prawns to the dish and leave for 3 - 5 minutes, until the rice is soft and excess water has evaporated. You don't want this to be too dry but you do not want it to be too runny either.

Serve with a slice of lemon.

PATSY'S CALLOS

THIS RECIPE
SERVES 12

COOKING TIME
8 HOURS

Callos are full of flavour and a great hearty meal to feed the whole family with. Slow cooked to perfection this is not a dish for the faint hearted.

INGREDIENTS

- 1.5 KG CALLOS (TRIPE)
- 1 PIGS TROTTER (CUT IN QUARTERS)
- 50 G BUTTER
- 1/2 PKT DRIED CHICKPEAS*
- 1/2 HEAD OF GARLIC
- 250 G ONIONS
- 50 G TOCINO (BELLY PORK)
- 50 G UNSMOKED BACON
- 50 G CHORIZO
- 50 G MORCILLA (BLOOD PUDDING)
- 1/2 KG TOMATOES
- 3 CLOVES
- 1 TSP PIMENTON (SMOKED PAPRIKA)
- LOOSE LEAF PARSELY
- HIERBABUENA (SPEARMINT LEAVES)
- SALT
- PEPPER
- 150 ML WATER

Soak your chickpeas overnight.

LET'S COOK

1. Begin by thoroughly rinsing your callos and trotters and placining them in a slow cooker. Add the rest of your ingredients to the pan, try not to cut them too big as they are easier to eat and serve this way and place your slow cooker over a medium heat.

2. Add your fresh, soaked chickpeas to the pot and cover everything with the water and a generous pinch of salt and pepper. *(Use fresh chickpeas as pre-soaked will not have the same consistency and may turn to mush).*

3. Bring everything to a boil, cover and simmer for 8 hours, stirring occasionally and topping up with water as necessary, to allow everything to cook well, soften and the flavours to bind. Taste when ready and season if necessary.

4. Should you prefer, you could also place your pot in the oven for 8 hours at 100°C.

Recipe By Patsy Felices

NOTE
Chorizo and chickpea quantites can be doubled to include more or as stated in the list.

MAMA'S POTAJE DE COLES
MAMA'S CABBAGE STEW

THIS RECIPE
SERVES 5

COOKING TIME
1 HOUR

Very similar to the Potaje de Berza found in Mama's previous cookbook, the Potaje de Coles, instead is made with cabbage rather than runner beans giving the stew a whole new taste.

INGREDIENTS

- 500 G PORK COLLAR
- 500 G STEWING STEAK
- 1 PIG'S TROTTER
- 110 G PORK BELLY
- 110 G BLACK PUDDING
- 110 G CHORIZO
- 1/2 KG CABBAGE
- 2 GARLIC CLOVES
- 1 MEDIUM ONION
- 2 FRESH TOMATOES
- 1 LARGE PUMPKIN SLICE
- 5 POTATOES
- 400 G BUTTER BEANS
- 400 G CHICKPEAS
- 1 TSP PAPRIKA
- 8 WHOLE BLACK
- PEPPERCORNS
- 1 TSP CUMIN POWDER

LET'S COOK

1. In a pressure cooker, place your pork collar, stewing steak, pig's trotter, pork belly, chorizo, whole, peeled garlic cloves, one onion cut in two, tomatoes cut in two, pumpkin, chopped mint, teaspoon of paprika, eight whole black peppercorns and one teaspoon of cumin powder.

2. Cover your ingredients with boiling water and season with salt. This should take 45 minutes in a pressure cooker, or alternatively cook until tender in a casserole dish, continually topping up with water.

3. Once everything is tender, remove the meat, pig's trotters and chorizo and blend the remaining vegetables. Add your chopped up cabbage, chickpeas, butter beans, black pudding and potatoes to your blended pan. Cook for 15 minutes in a pressure cooker and remove from the heat.

   Alternatively, place in a casserole dish, partially covered for 30 - 40 minutes or until tender, topping up with water as required.

4. Place your meat and chorizo back in with all your ingredients once everything is tender and soft.

BECHAMEL CROQUETTES
WITH LEFTOVER TURKEY

THIS RECIPE
SERVES 5
COOKING TIME
30 MINUTES

Croquettes or 'croquetas' as they are also more commonly known in Gibraltar are the perfect solution to leftovers. Quick to make and easily consumed, these are perfect for kids or as a tapas at lunch.

INGREDIENTS

- 200 G GRATED CHEESE
- 3 TBSP FLOUR
- 500 ML MILK
- NUTMEG
- CHICKEN CUBE
- 60 G BREADCRUMBS
- 3 EGGS
- MARJORAM
- SALT
- PEPPER
- 1 ONION
- 120 G BITS OF BACON *(OPTIONAL)*
- 120 G TURKEY *(OPTIONAL)*
- 120 G SPANISH HAM *(OPTIONAL)*

LET'S COOK

1. Fry your onion, add cooked, meat and 3 tablespoons of flour, start adding milk flavoured with a pinch of nutmeg, half chicken cube, salt and pepper, a little grated cheese and mix until forming a ball in the centre of the pan. The aim is to make a very thick béchamel sauce. Slowly adding flour to the mix to thicken as required.

2. Once the béchamel is ready, stir and pour into an oven dish to cool down. Allow this to cool, then place in the fridge to allow it to reach a consistency where you are able to mould it.

3. Once thick and ready, prepare the croquettes by rolling them into small balls or whatever shape and size you fancy.

4. In two separate bowls, prepare one with a whisked egg, mix together with a very finely chopped garlic and parsley. In the other pour out a plate of breadcrumbs.

5. Dip your croquettes in each, egg first, and fry until golden brown.

Recipe By Ana Maria Morro

HAM AND PRAWNS LINGUINE

THIS RECIPE

SERVES 1

COOKING TIME

20 MINUTES

I love seafood and I may have a slight obsession with serrano ham, especially during the holidays... I mean it's just unnatural, no one should consume that much ham. Anyway that aside, here's a dish that combines two of my favourite foods into one tasty afternoon dish.

INGREDIENTS

- 56 G LINGUINE

- SERRANO HAM CHUNKS

- 1 GARLIC CLOVE

- 250 G PRAWNS

- PARMESAN CHEESE

- TOMATO PESTO

- SPINACH *(OPTIONAL)*

- MUSHROOMS *(OPTIONAL)*

LET'S COOK

1. Place linguine in boiling water.

2. Finely dice the garlic and mushrooms and fry in a pan over a medium heat with a tablespoon of oil.

3. When the garlic is soft, add the prawns until thoroughly cooked.

4. Add the ham pieces and a teaspoon of tomato pesto. Chop some spinach and add to the pan should you wish to add it.

5. When the pasta is ready, drain and add to the pan. Stir and mix everything together.

6. Sprinkle with parmesan cheese and serve.

CIMA RELLENA
STUFFED FLANK STEAK

SERVES 4

- - - - - - - - - - - - - - -

COOKING TIME

2 HOURS

A tender and succulent piece of beef stuffed with mama's delicious stuffing mix, roasted and served up as thin slices. A great Sunday roast alternative.

INGREDIENTS

- 1 KG
  FLANK STEAK

- 3 EGGS

- PARSLEY

- 2 GARLIC CLOVES

- GRATED CHEESE

- BREADCRUMBS

LET'S COOK

1. Ask your butcher to carefully slice a pocket in the beef skirt or flank steak when purchasing, alternatively you can do this yourself.

2. Mix three eggs, parsley, chopped garlic, grated cheese and breadcrumbs together.

3. Stuff it all into the opening of the beef skirt, leaving some space within as the stuffing will expand when cooking.

4. Close the opening by sewing it together or held together with cocktail sticks.

5. Line an oven dish and prepare your meat by wrapping it up in foil paper and placing it in the oven at 200°C for about 2 hours.

Alternatively, you can cook the meat in a soup, chop a selection of vegetables and place in a pressure cooker or casserole, covered with water until the meat is tender. This should take between 40 minutes to 1 hour 15 minutes.

MAMA'S SAN JACOBO
GRANNY'S CORDON BLEU

THIS RECIPE

SERVES 2

COOKING TIME
35 MINUTES

I always remember having these as a kid, so deliciously tender, with melted cheese pouring out as you cut into it...yummy!

INGREDIENTS

- 2 CHICKEN BREAST FILLETS
- SMOKED HAM
- MATURE CHEDDAR CHEESE
- BREADCRUMBS
- FLOUR
- 2 EGGS
- PARSLEY
- 1 GARLIC CLOVE

LET'S COOK

1. Preheat oven to 190 °C.

2. Slice your two chicken breast fillets in half into slightly thinner slices.

3. Cut a pocket into your chicken breast fillet and fill with cheese and ham.

4. Sear the chicken in a hot pan so that the outside is just cooked and the inside remains raw. This will ensure that the chicken remains juicy when cooking in the oven.

5. Remove from the pan onto a plate and allow the chicken to cool. Whilst the chicken cools, finely chop some parsley and the garlic clove and mix this with your beaten eggs. Proceed to bread the chicken by covering with flour, into the egg and into the breadcrumbs.

6. Place the chicken pieces in an oven dish and cook in the oven for 30 – 45 minutes, until thoroughly cooked and golden.

7. I boiled some simple white rice to go with it.

MAMA'S PATATA A LO POBRE
GRANNY'S POOR MAN'S POTATOES

Growing up, this was one of my favourite mama side dishes. This quick and easy recipe goes well with any meat and fish dish. It may appear simple but it's full of flavour and texture.

INGREDIENTS

- 10 BABY POTATOES OR 4 MEDIUM POTATOES
- 1 ONION
- 2 LONG GREEN PEPPERS
- SALT
- PEPPER
- OIL

LET'S COOK

1. Thinly slice your potatoes and fry in a pan with a little oil, salt and pepper.

2. Slice the onion and peppers lengthways and add to the pan, along with your potatoes and cover.

3. Leave your pan on a medium heat. *Covering the pan fries the vegetables but also boils them in their own steam, softening the potatoes.*

4. This should take about 20 minutes. Stir occasionally until soft and season to taste.

MAMA'S CLAM LINGUINE
A SIMPLE CLAM PASTA DISH

THIS RECIPE
SERVES 2
- - - - - - - - - - - - - - - -
COOKING TIME
15 MINUTES

Do we need a reason to enjoy seafood? I'm such a fan of clams I decided to use the 'Almejas al Ajillo' as inspiration for this meal.

INGREDIENTS

- TWO HANDFULS LINGUINE
- 450 G CLAMS
- 1 FRYING GREEN PEPPER
- 2 GARLIC CLOVES
- PARSLEY

LET'S COOK

1. Firstly, make sure to soak your clams in water for several hours before you begin, to remove any sand inside them.

2. Steam your clams by placing them in a large covered pan over a medium heat for 10 minutes.

3. In the meantime, chop some garlic and very finely dice the peppers into very small pieces.

4. Fry these in an iron griddled pan and pour the clams into the pan. Now, boil some pasta until they soften.

5. After several minutes your clams should almost be ready, they will all have opened. Sprinkle over with a pinch or two of parsley and leave for a further minute or two.

6. Drain your pasta and add this to the pan with your clams, stir and mix everything together, season with a pinch of salt and allow any excess liquid to evaporate.

AUNTY'S STUFFED PEPPERS
WITH MINCED MEAT IN A TOMATO SAUCE

THIS RECIPE

SERVES 4

COOKING TIME

40 MINUTES

Peppers are great things to cook with, with so many ways to prepare them. Fry, roast or steam...so if you want a great meal without too much effort try these stuffed peppers. They could even be made vegetarian.

INGREDIENTS

- 500 G MINCED MEAT

- 800 G TOMATE TITURADO OR PASSATA

- 12 FRYING GREEN PEPPERS *(3 PER PERSON)*

- 1 MEDIUM ONION

- 2 GARLIC CLOVES

- 1 TSP OREGANO

- SALT

- PEPPER

- CHEESE

LET'S COOK

1. Finely chop the onion and garlic and fry in a little oil until soft and translucent.

2. Once soft, add in the minced meat and season with a bit of salt, pepper and oregano.

3. Stir until the meat is thoroughly cooked and pour the tin of tomatoes over. Leave to stew for a few minutes.

4. Meanwhile, rinse and clean out your peppers by removing the head and taking out any seeds, leaving the rest of the pepper intact.

5. Remove your pan from the heat and begin to carefully scoop spoonfuls of the meat mixture into the peppers.

6. Lay your stuffed peppers on an oven dish and spread the remaining tomato sauce over. Grate and cover with cheese.

7. Place this in the oven at 200°C for 30 - 40 minutes, until the peppers have softened and the cheese turns golden.

Recipe By Janet Laguea

MUM'S PEPPERED STEAK

THIS RECIPE
SERVES 2

COOKING TIME
20 MINUTES

Mum's creamed peppered steak sauce has always been a favourite of mine. So creamy and moreish you will end up licking the plate clean, so have some bread nearby.

INGREDIENTS

- 500G BEEF STEAK
- SMALL DOUBLE CREAM
- BLACK PEPPERCORN
- GROUND BLACK PEPPER
- BEEF STOCK CUBE
- SALT
- DOLLOP OF BUTTER
- SHOT BRANDY OR COGNAC *(OPTIONAL)*

LET'S COOK

1. Slice your beef into long thin strips and season with black pepper and salt and fry until browned in a dollop of butter.

2. Whilst frying your meat, add your beef stock and the peppercorns.

3. Once the beef is cooked to your liking, add the double cream and if you have any, a shot of brandy or cognac. Stir the mixture.

4. Taste your sauce, if you would like it more peppery and spicy just add more ground pepper in small quantities and stir.

5. Fry some chips or boil some rice and serve.

SWEETS

TORTILLAS DE PASAS
FRIED AND GLAZED RASIN BITES

We love raisins and sweet things. Mama's Tortillas de Pasas are soft and sticky. Perfect for tea time.

INGREDIENTS

- 225 G SELF-RAISING FLOUR

- 236 ML WATER

- 2 TBSP SUGAR

- 1 SHOT BRANDY

- 110 G RAISINS

- CINNAMON

- GOLDEN SYRUP

- OIL TO FRY

LET'S COOK

1. Create the mixture by sifting the flour into a bowl, adding in the sugar, water, mixing everything together.

2. Add the shot of brandy and raisins and continue to mix together well.

3. Heat some oil in a frying pan and pour in a couple of spoonfuls of the mixture at a time.

4. Fry your tortillas, turning over after a minute or two to cook the opposite side. Once all your mixture is done, leave to one side over kitchen paper to drain any excess oil and heat up the golden syrup.

5. Dip each torta into the syrup, covering generously and place in a container or dish. Finish off by sprinkling over with cinnamon.

PASTELITOS DE
CABELLO DE ANGEL

THIS RECIPE
SERVES 8

COOKING TIME
15 MINUTES

These sweet treats are more filling than they appear. Light and fluffy pastry surrounding sweet and sticky pumpkin jam.

LET'S COOK

- 500 G PUFF PASTRY

- 1 TIN CABELLO DE ANGEL

- 1 EGG TO GLAZE

- CASTOR SUGAR TO DECORATE

1. Roll the pastry into round shapes, place some cabello de Angel in the middle and fold the pastry over.

2. Place on a baking tray and brush with a beaten egg.

3. Oven for 10 - 15 minutes at 200°C.

4. Once golden and puffed, remove from the oven, decorate with some castor sugar and leave to cool.

Recipe By Rose Carter

MAMA LOTTIES - TASTING THE MEDITERRANEAN

HOJUELAS

A FRIED, FLAKE LIKE TREAT

THIS RECIPE

SERVES 6

COOKING TIME

10 MINUTES

These are a bit tricky to do, but get them right and you'll have a lovely, crumbly flake to enjoy with friends.

INGREDIENTS

- 3 EGGS

- 3 HALF EGG SHELLS OF OIL

- 400 G PLAIN FLOUR

- HUNDREDS & THOUSANDS

- 400 G SUGAR

- 200 ML WARM WATER

- ANISE LIQUEUR *(TWO SHOTS)*

LET'S COOK

1. Whisk together 3 egg whites and yolks, with 3 half egg shells of oil, then add the flour. Once you have a dough like substance, roll this out very thinly and slice into wide rectangular strips, about 4 cm wide and 10 cm length.

2. Place these to one side and prepare your syrup. Melt the sugar in the water and two shots of anise, depending how strong you prefer the taste.

3. Once the sauce is ready, leave to one side to cool and heat up a frying pan with oil. Now carefully, place a strip at a time into the oil and fry. Whilst you are frying, using a pair of forks, roll the pastry into a cylinder, so that it keeps its shape once ready, without breaking.

4. Once fried, place each piece on a plate with kitchen paper so as to drain any excess oil and allow to cool. Finally dip each flake into the syrup and cover generously. Finish off by sprinkling over hundreds and thousands.

Recipe By Rose Carter

MAMA LOTTIES - TASTING THE MEDITERRANEAN

YEMITAS DE HUEVOS
SWEET EGG YOLKS

THIS RECIPE

SERVES 3

COOKING TIME
30 MINUTES

Heat, stir, roll and powder. It can take some time to get the consistency right but in the end it's worth the time it takes.

INGREDIENTS

- 6 EGG YOLKS

- 100 G SUGAR

- 70 ML WATER

- ICING SUGAR

LET'S COOK

1. Separate your egg yolks into a bowl and beat together. Boil sugar and water in a pan until it's syrupy. Add the egg yolks to the pan, constantly stirring whilst it is over the heat until it thickens into a paste. This could take some time.

2. Remove from heat and let it cool down.

3. Using a teaspoon, scoop a bit of the egg paste and mould into balls. *I placed mine in the fridge, once moulded, for 5 - 10 minutes to harden further and help keep their shape.*

4. Once moulded and ready, generously sprinkle over with icing sugar and roll them over the sugar to smooth out the balls.

5. Serve them on a cake dish or in cupcake cases.

Recipe By Rose Carter

MAMA LOTTIES - TASTING THE MEDITERRANEAN

BESOS

I'm a big fan of almonds and these tiny macaroon-like bites are so tasty you might just end up eating them all yourself.

INGREDIENTS

- 100 G GROUND ALMONDS

- 100 G SUGAR

- 100 G BISCOCHO PLANTILLA OR *(BOUDOIR BISCUITS)*

- 1 WHOLE EGG

- 2 SHOTS OF "LICOR 43"

CUSTARD SYRUP

- 3 EGG YOLKS

- 100 G SUGAR

LET'S COOK

1. Mash up the Boudoir Biscuits, and mix with the egg, the sugar, the ground almonds and 2 shots of "Licor 43"

2. When this is ready make small balls with this mixture and flatten in the palm of your hands, keeping your hands slightly cupped.

3. Lay these out on a baking tray and place under a medium grill for about 2 minutes. Just enough so that they dry out a bit but still remain soft. Allow them to cool on a baking rack.

4. In the meantime make a syrup with 100G of sugar and enough water to cover the sugar and the base of the pan. Heat until the sugar is dissolved. When this is ready leave it to cool.

5. Whisk 3 egg yolks and mix with the syrup. Place the pan back on a low heat stirring all the time until it thickens... It should be a custard-like consistency.

6. Butter the sides of the Besos with the egg mixture, pour a bit on the flat side of one facing up and sandwich together, finish off with a sprinkle of cinnamon

Recipe By Dorothy Victory-Aleman

ROSCO DE ANIS

THIS RECIPE
SERVES 8
- - - - - - - - - - - - - - - - -
COOKING TIME
45 MINUTES

Anise can be strong so go easy on the syrup otherwise it won't just be 'don't drink and drive' but 'don't eat and drive'.

INGREDIENTS

CAKE

- 255 G SUGAR

- 255 G SELF RAISING FLOUR

- 6 EGGS

SYRUP

- 350 ML WATER

- 250 G SUGAR

- 250 ML ANISE

- CINNAMON

LET'S COOK

1. Beat the egg yolks together with the sugar, leaving the egg whites seperately to one side.

2. Once the eggs and sugar are creamed together, mix in the flour. Make sure not to over mix, but just enough to blend the contents together.

3. Leave to one side and beat the egg white until you have a peaked merringue. Now fold this into your batter, until all the egg white and batter is blended together.

4. Place your batter in a lined bunt tin and bake at 180°C for 40 to 45 minutes.

5. Once golden and fluffy and you see that you can pierce your cake and have a clean blade, leave to one side to cool and prepare your syrup.

6. Heat the water and sugar in a pan until everything is dissolved and reduces, then add your anise.

7. When cool, flip your cake over and pour half the syrup over the bottom of the cake, allow to soak for a few minutes, then flip and repeat over the top. Finish off with a sprinkle of cinnamon.

PAN DULCE

MAWISA'S SWEET BREAD

SERVES 6

COOKING TIME
40 MINUTES

Perfect during christmas, this is a sweet bread that is traditionally enjoyed during the festive season and ideal with a cup of tea.

INGREDIENTS

- 300 G SELF RAISING FLOUR
- 125 G SUGAR
- 125 G MARGARINE
- 1 TSP BAKING POWDER
- 125 G MIXED FRUIT
- 50 G GLACÉ CHERRIES
- 50 G WALNUTS
- 50 G PINENUTS
- 2 LARGE EGGS
- 100 ML MILK
- 1 TSP DRY ANISE
- HUNDREDS & THOUSANDS
- GOLDEN SYRUP
- 50 G ALMONDS
- 50 G MIXED PEEL

LET'S COOK

1. Using the rubbing method, rub together the flour, sugar and margarine in a large bowl using your fingertips until it resembles breadcrumbs.

2. Add all the fruits and nuts and mix in with your mixture

3. Now continue by adding in the wet ingredients such as the eggs, milk and dry anise and stir together with a wooden spoon, until mixed well.

4. You should now have a nice dough consistency to knead with. Knead the dough into the shape of a loaf; with this mixture you can make one very large loaf or two medium loaves.

5. Finish your preparation by brushing your loaves over with milk and using a knife criss-crossing the top. Bake in the oven at 180 °C for 30 - 40 minutes.

6. Remove from oven when ready. Poke several holes throughout the top and brush over with golden syrup, finish off by sprinkling hundreds and thousands all over.

Recipe By Mawisa

MAMA'S TARTA DE SANTIAGO
ALMOND TART

THIS RECIPE
SERVES 8

COOKING TIME
60 MINUTES

This Galician tart has made its way into my kitchen from the north of Spain. However, I gave this my own little twist with Licor 43 and orange zest.

INGREDIENTS

- 4 EGGS
- 250 G UNREFINED SUGAR
- 1 TSP CINNAMON
- 250G GROUND ALMONDS
- 50 G BUTTER
- 1 SHOT 'LICOR 43'
- ORANGE ZEST
- ICING SUGAR

LET'S COOK

1. Preheat oven to 200 °C.

2. Mix the eggs and sugar in a large bowl until creamed and fluffy. When you reach the right consistency, add in the almonds, cinnamon, butter, orange zest and liqueur.

3. Mix everything together into a smooth paste and pour into a greased, spring base cake tin.

4. Transfer into the oven and leave for 1 hour, checking that the cake is golden and crisp on top and softer inside.

PAN DE NUEZ

MAWISA'S WALNUT BREAD

SERVES 5

COOKING TIME

45 MINUTES

Bread is delicious so when you make it sweet and add some nuts it just gets even better.

INGREDIENTS

- 450 G SELF RAISING FLOUR
- 280 ML MILK
- 150 G SEEDLESS RAISINS
- 150 G WALNUTS
- 150 G CASTER SUGAR
- 2 EGGS
- 2 TBSP BUTTER
- 1 TSP BAKING POWDER
- DASH OF CINNAMON

LET'S COOK

1. Place raisins and walnuts in a dish and cover with milk. Leave for at least one to two hours to soak.

2. Beat eggs, sugar, butter and cream together then slowly add in the sifted self raising flour and baking powder and mix everything together.

3. Add the mixture of nuts and stir all together until you have a thick and creamy texture, add a dash of cinnamon to your mix.

4. Transfer your batter into a buttered loaf tin and place in the oven for 40 - 45 minutes at 180°C.

Recipe By Mawisa

AMARETTO FLAN TRIFLE

THIS RECIPE
SERVES 3

PREPARATION TIME
15 MINUTES

Fruit trifle is always a great dessert after a full meal. Usually soaked in anise, these instead were soaked in amaretto and covered with a peach and banana custard. Try them your own way.

INGREDIENTS

- 2 BANANAS

- 1 TIN PEACH SLICES

- 1 PACKET CRÈME CARAMEL *(FLAN)* POWDER

- 1 PINT MILK

- 1 PACKET BOUDOIRS *(SPONGE FINGERS)*

- 1 SHOT OF AMARETTO LIQUEUR

- CHOCOLATE

LET'S COOK

I used 3 wine glasses but a medium glass dish would do.

1. This recipe is all about creating layers. Begin by placing the boudoirs at the bottom, slice your banana and lay them over the biscuit, do the same with the peach slices. You should be able to create two if not 3 layers.

2. Save the peach juice and mix this with your amaretto liqueur, stir and pour over your fruit. This will sink to the bottom and be absorbed by the biscuits. Anise, brandy or any other liqueur will work just as well.

3. Pour your pint of milk into a measuring jug and heat in the microwave for 3 minutes. Remove and stir then add your crème caramel powder, stir and mix well and place back in the microwave for 3 more minutes.

4. Once ready, remove stir and place to one side for a minute. Pour the mixture evenly over your dessert and allow to cool. This should begin to set after a while. Once cooler place in the fridge for a few hours until it has fully set.

5. Finish off by grating some chocolate over the top

INDEX

Made in the USA
Charleston, SC
24 November 2015